Garden Flowers

Sean McCann

Illustrated by
BRIDGET FLINN

Appletree Press

First published in 1995 by
The Appletree Press Ltd
19–21 Alfred Street, Belfast BT2 8DL
Tel: +44 (0) 1232 243074 Fax: +44 (0) 1232 246756
Copyright © 1995 The Appletree Press, Ltd.
Printed in the E.U. All rights reserved.

A Little Book of Garden Flowers

A catalogue record for this book is available
in The British Library.

ISBN 0-86281-529-0

9 8 7 6 5 4 3 2 1

The flowers on these pages have a long and glorious history; beautiful, magical and peaceful, the flowers of yesterday have been brought a long way from their originals by world plant breeders but they retain their classic attributes and today are still very much a part of gardens everywhere.

They are limitless in their number and variety. They bring their unique colours, textures, growth habits, fragrance and foliage to the garden. Without flowers, wrote William Robinson, the father of English gardens, in *The English Flower Garden* (1883), our gardens and our lives would be as 'bare of life as a piece of oilcloth'.

Whether they are grown in a small container on a patio or balcony or left to drift unchecked in a large garden, these flowers bring solace, memories, pleasure and peace with them. Flowers can dumbfound even the most hardened pessimist.

You will find the words beautiful, magical, wonderful used frequently in my descriptions in this little book. That is how I find flowers. I have a personal affection for each of the twenty-eight flowers that I have selected – from forget-me-nots to the wild valerian – reminding me of Tennyson's words:

> Flower in the crannied wall,
> I pluck you out of the crannies,
> I hold you here, root and all, in my hand,
> Little Flower – but if I could understand
> What you are, root and all, all in all,
> I should know what God and man is.

Sean McCann

The anemone is a princely little flower that might be better recognised if it were called the old name of "windflower". The superb artist Redouté painted it with a velvet bloom and a dewy tear on its petals. Its flowers are coloured red and royal purple, pastel pink and white, lavender and mauve, sometimes streaked with a wonderful grouping of stamens. It is part of a large family of some one hundred and fifty different species, some tuberous rooted, others rhizomatous. Most species sold by seed merchants are of the double St Brigid or single De Caen types; the flowers brighten many spring homes when bought from corner flower-sellers but garden plants need to be kept warm and well nurtured. They also need to be replaced every two years or so as they deteriorate. While there are individual varieties within these groups – such as the blue Mr Fokker, white The Bride (De Caen), magenta The Admiral and scarlet The Governor (St. Brigid) – most of them can be purchased in mixed collections.

The Japanese anemone is very much at home in most herbaceous borders. It has large 2–3 inch flowers on plants that can be 4 ft/1.2m high, and blooms from August to October. William Robinson, who wrote *The English Garden* at the beginning of this century, mentioned Honorine Jobert from this group and its pure white flowers adorn a beautiful plant frequently recommended by breeders to gardeners. The wild wood anemone adorns the woodlands of England, Europe and parts of Asia. It can be grown effectively in rock gardens. The Anemone Blanda, originating in the hills of Greece, blooms from February to April in both white and pastel shades of blue and mauve pink.

In a world of exotic lilies, radiant roses, dainty violas and perky pinks the humble antirrhinum seems outclassed and in these days of changing attractions has even gone out of fashion. Perhaps it has become too familiar. However, it is one of the most ancient of garden flowers. The "Snapdragon" (*A. magus*) collection especially catches the attention. It is a half-hardy annual which, with luck, will go on and on repeatedly seeding itself in your garden for many years. It need not have good soil (but, of course, does better in well-cultivated ground) and, where it has been allowed freedom, can often be found growing annually on walls and poor ground. The name is Greek, meaning 'like a nose or snout' and in some areas it has been called "Calf's Snout" and even "Weasel's Snout". The name by which it is best known is "Snapdragon" as the long snout looks like that of a dragon. How many children have had the fun and excitement of seeing the "jaws" or side of the corolla being pinched open to reveal a tooth-like interior?

Not many gardeners would name the antirrhinum as one of their favourite flowers, though Gertrude Jekyll, one of the worl's great garden makers and writers at the turn of the century (1843–1932), named it as one of hers. It might still have been among the most popular of garden flowers had it not fallen victim to rust disease which attacked the old varieties some years ago. However, plant breeders have managed to raise new varieties with a measure of resistance to the disease. There are also some good fungicides that provide protection. The varieties of antirrhinum that filled gardens of old with flowers from June to the first frosts can still be enjoyed. To encourage bushiness, pinch out the centres of young plants, and to prolong the flowering period remove the faded blooms.

It comes as something of a surprise to find that a flower
carrying such a definitive name as Bells of Ireland should come
originally from Western Asia and, certainly, it has no real
historical or botanical association with Ireland. The plant gets
its name from the fact that it is green and white, colours long
associated with Ireland, but it does not receive any national
honour or special place in the gardens of that country. It is, in
fact, one of four species in the Molucella group of Shell-
flowers, and is frequently named as a Mediterranean herb.
The leaves are carried in a tuft above and below the 12 inch/
30 cm long flower spike, while the flowers are small white
blooms wrapped around by a large, shell-like pale green calyx.

Over the years it has not been given much glory as a garden
plant. Some writers have called it dull, uninteresting,
insignificant and colourless but others, mainly those with an
interest in flower arranging, find that it is endlessly useful. Its
real beauty is as a cut flower in arrangements and as a flower
for winter decoration when the white flowers and the foliage
can be detached to leave the green calyx.

It isn't an easy plant to get started and seed should be sown
as a hardy annual in a warm March or April, thinning out the
plants as they grow. Alternatively, the seedlings can be grown
in a warm greenhouse and then hardened off in a cold frame
before planting out. The plants do their best in light rich soil
in a sunny open position and will grow to over 2 ft/60 cm high.
When they do start growing, they are trouble free.

This is not strictly a flowering plant, it is more like a shrub and sometimes grows to the size of a small tree. The flowers are fragrant, slender and tubular but the most attractive attribute of the buddleia is its encouragement of butterflies. Indeed, the most general name of the widely planted *B. davidii* is "butterfly bush". At times in the summer the delicate and fragrant long, arching plume shaped clusters of bloom can be covered with butterflies. *B. davidii* originated in China and makes a wide, strong growing shrub with lilac purple flowers in dense clusters from July to October. It has an evocative perfume and can be found growing wild today with almost the same vigour as the valerian plant.

There are many new varieties available within the *B. davidii* grouping in colours of dark violet-purple, blue with an orange eye, rich-red purple and white. The family is a large one with over one hundred species distributed throughout Asia, Europe and America. They belong to the genus Buddleja, a name given to them by Linneaus to honour an English vicar from Essex, the Rev. Adam Buddle, who died in 1715.

Among the other notable varieties is the *B. globosa*, often known as the orange ball tree. It comes from Chile, has fragrant orange-yellow balls of bloom and needs a mild climate to be seen at its best.

The buddleia family is generally a hardy one. Plants can be cut back with determination only for it to spiritedly rise again next summer. *B. globosa*, however, needs only light pruning as it produces blossoms on the previous year's wood. Propagation is by heel cuttings of half-hardy lateral shoots while *B. davidii* can easily be increased by hardwood cuttings taken in October and planted outside.

❧ Cabbage Rose ❧

The cabbage rose is a large, full-petalled pink rose that has scented our gardens for generations. Indeed, it is by the cabbage rose that most other varieties are judged for their fragrance. Its botanical name is *Rosa x centifolia* – the hundred-leaved rose. The head is large and full but there the resemblance with a cabbage ends. The father of England's roses, Reverend Dean Hole (1819–1904), declared the name an outrage for such a beautiful rose. The *centifolia* is loved by gardeners and by painters. In her magnificent book, *Rose at the Cape of Good Hope*, Gwen Fagan wrote that she had examined prints of four hundred European paintings covering the period 1600–1900 and sixty-six per cent of these featured a *centifolia*. For many years it was considered to be the oldest of roses, the scented rose of Herodotus, but recent research has shown that it really is not old by rose standards, probably being developed in the sixteenth century by Dutch growers.

It was called the Provence rose because of its widespread use in France, although in 1597 John Gerard called it "the Holland or Provence rose". Gertrude Jekyll in *Roses for English Gardens* (1901) said: "No rose surpasses it in excellence of scent; it stands alone as the sweetest of its kind, as the type of true Rose smell." Rose G. Kingsley in *Roses and Rose Growing* (1908) wrote: "In spite of all newcomers, beautiful and attractive as they are, the old Cabbage Rose holds its own today in the garden of every true rose-lover, as unsurpassed in fragrance and colour." In gardens it must be given room to develop with room for the lax, lanky growth to find its own placing. Like all roses, it enjoys sunshine and glows with health and vigour when well cared for in a good humus rich soil. It will reach some $6^1/_2$ ft/2m in height.

Canterbury Bells bring to mind an old English cottage garden. Blooming from May to July, the plant has bell-shaped flowers that can be both single, semi-single and double. The plants are quite at home in the country garden setting, being both showy and distinct as they grow as high as 30 inches/76cm. Some varieties stay at about 15 inches/38cm high with pyramids of blooms. The problem with Canterbury Bells for modern gardeners is that the plant tends to die after the flowering period (May to July) and, if it has grown too large, leaves large gaps in borders. This can be overcome by planting in small groups in a well-foliaged area.

Canterbury Bells should have been lost in the huge selection of the Campanula family to which it belongs (C. *medium*) but no doubt was saved by pilgrims' sentiments. Its name comes from its resemblance to St Thomas's Bells, small brass bells sold as badges to pilgrims at the shrine of St Thomas à Becket in Canterbury Cathedral, and it is still known as the bellflower.

It comes in many colours – white, mauve, purple, rose and blue. The one remembered from the old gardens is the pink type, truly bell shaped with exquisite flowers. A sturdy, upright plant with bright, hairy and wavy-toothed leaves, it grows best in sun or partial shade in fertile, well-drained soil. Dead-heading the plants will ensure that the flowering period lasts as long as possible.

One of the world's most social – and scented – flowers. Famed for its clove-like scent, it was the popular buttonhole filler for gentlemen of the 1920s. It is still the favoured flower for wedding decoration and one of the cheeriest of all flowers. After the rose, wrote William Robinson in *The English Garden* "should come the carnation, in all its brilliancy of colour – the laced, the striped and the flaked … we should show the flower in all its force of colour in our gardens." Both Gertrude Jekyll and Robinson would, no doubt, have had little trouble in using the name given to the carnation by the ancient Greeks – "The Divine Flower". Jekyll talked of it as the flower "with the firmest hold on the gardener's heart" but wondered why the old name, the Gilliflower (derived from *giroflée*, the French word for clove), a name often used by Elizabethan poets, had gone out of use even then. Shakespeare wrote that "the fairest flowers o' the season are our carnations".

Growing records go back some four hundred years while flower studies by many Old Masters such as Holbein and Rembrandt frequently place the carnation in a prominent spot. In the seventeenth century the flower was recognised by the earliest of garden writers, John Parkinson, who devoted a whole chapter to it in his *Paradisus Terrestris*. Even then there were some fifty known varieties.

While generally called "pinks" today (carnations come in many other colours) there are many hundreds of varieties from small miniatures to those that are allowed to grow into small hedges. The flowering period is mainly through June and July and they do need a good soil in which to thrive.

Its massed and magnificent flowers makes clematis romantic and beautiful enough to be called the "Virgin's Bower". There is no climbing plant in the whole of the flower kingdom to compare. The Greeks called all climbing plants "clematis" and it was from this description that the plant took its name. It certainly is a great climber and many varieties harbour Everest-like ambitions that send them sweeping over trees and other obstacles with impunity. A high flier such as C. *montana*, a pure white clematis from the Himalayas, is so vigorous that it will almost obscure a tree. Other varieties are content to grow to eye level like the lavender blue hybrid "Lasurstern" and the lovely and widely planted "Nellie Moser" with its pale pink and carmine striped flowers. There is a clematis for every part of the garden and for every season of the year. Some plants are evergreen, others deciduous. Some have small blooms, some flowers are shaped like bells, urns and stars; others are large, dramatic circular blooms.

Probably the most popular of all clematis is *Jackmanii Superba*, with its velvet, dark purple, white-eyed enormous blooms that make their show in late summer and continue flowering until first frost. They range in colour from the pure white to purple, red, blue and even yellow; there are bicolours also, as in C. *florida* whose inner petals are purple with white outer parts. A clematis may need help to become established but once it is set well in the ground the foliage takes over and the long stalks of the leaves wrap themselves around any support. The plants thrive in an average soil but must have good drainage and their roots should be shaded from the sun.

Fanciful, fickle, whimsical – the lovely, old-fashioned columbine has had all kinds of descriptions through the years. But there are few plants quite as charming or as easy to raise as, when left to their own devices, their seeds can be blown by the wind to grow anywhere in the garden. A damp, warm but not hot, border seems to be ideal for their growth. The flowers range in colour from white, rose and many shades of blue and purples, and, indeed, many other shades have appeared from hybrid seeds. The widest variety of colours is in the *A. vulgaris* which is often known as "Granny's Bonnet" because of the unusual spurred and funnel shaped blooms, each with extravagant five petals which suggested to the poet Jean Ingelow the line "O Columbine, open your folded wrapper".

The McKana Hybrids and the Mrs Scott-Elliot's Strain have a large range of colours – cream, yellow, pink, red, crimson and blue flowers. These varieties will grow to some 3 ft/90cm high and flower in early summer. There are also alpine species which grow 6 inches/15 cm high (the *A. bertononii* Italian variety with its rich blue flowers is a delight). Columbines are not happy to be moved as they form a taproot which is not easily dug up. It is better to collect and plant the profuse seeds. Plants will bloom from May to early July depending on the climate and when they rest in late summer they do so lazily and not very elegantly. However, this is a small price to pay for such a delightful flower.

❧ Cornflower ❧

The faults of the little cornflower are few, the virtues numerous. One of the oldest and best-loved garden flowers, it is a simple hardy annual with a few varieties available as perennials. When other plants around it are burgeoning with the weight of heavy blooms and sometimes impossible foliage, the small full thistle-like head of the cornflower blooms in unsophisticated sincerity. Once it was called the "Bluebottle", the "Blue Bothem" and the "Blue Knapweed". In Russia it was named "basilek" in memory of a young man, named Vassili, or Basil, loved by a nymph who took him to the fields of ripe corn and changed him into a plant so that he could never charm another. There are many other legends throughout Europe connected with the flower; additions to bridal bouquets of even a single cornflower are a trust in love; the goddess Flora took the body of a young poet and changed it into a cornflower so that his verses about the earth and its riches could always be remembered.

The name "cornflower" is said to be a translation of the Latin *flos frumenti* but its botanical name is really *Centaurea cyanus*. We think of the cornflower as blue but today it is available in red, yellow, pink and carmine, and even "milk chocolate" colour. Apothecaries have used it medicinally for hundreds of years, especially for eye troubles. It was also regarded as a good lotion for the face and the dried petals were used for gout, kidney troubles and rheumatism. It is an easy flower to grow, even in poor soils. Plants growing from self-sown seeds can be transplanted in the spring. If sown in September, the seeds last well through the hardest winters. The flowers are good for cutting.

ଓ Delphinium ଓ

Few flowers have advanced as much through the work of modern plant breeders as the delphinium. It has developed from a single-flowered variety in white and blue to a tall, handsome, theatrical presence that has a glorious array of colours. The delphiniums are a wonderful sight with their spires of bloom towering above soft, deeply cleft, often hairy foliage. William Robinson wrote about them in *The English Garden* (1883): "They are very valuable for their great variety in height, from one to ten feet; for their greater variety in shades of colour, which range from almost scarlet to pure white, from the palest and most chaste lavender through every conceivable shade of blue to deep indigo; and for the variety of size and form of their individual blooms, some of which are single, some semi-double, and all set on spikes ranging from one to six feet (30 cm–1.8 m) in height." The same is true today with a wider range of colour now available.

Though there are some two hundred known species, little is known of their origin. The cultivated plant is said to have arrived in Britain from either the Pyrenees or from Mongolia in the 1600s. Delphiniums grew wild in the cornfields of North America, and in Asia, Europe and North Africa. Its flowers were considered useful as a concoction for healing wounds and for alleviating eye complaints, while its seeds were used as a toothache cure and to treat spots and skin diseases. Belladonna (the name for a certain group of these plants) is still regarded as a lethal poison. Delphiniums can be grown relatively easily from seed sown where the plants are to bloom, but it is better to get a division of a good plant. The plants can be destroyed by mildew unless they are sprayed with a fungicide, and slugs are also an enemy.

The name "evening primrose" is a misnomer as the flower of this plant is more like a large saucer-shaped silky yellow poppy. North American settlers would have seen the plant in its natural habitat as they rolled their wagons westward through Utah, Missouri, Texas and California. The flowers show their true beauty at night. William Robinson called it "a large and charming moon; the most interesting flower I ever saw in a garden at night." There are some species that open during the day but it is best known as the evening primrose. Its botanical name is *Oenothera*, from the Greek.

The evening primrose is not only a gift to the gardener but also to those who practice holistic medicine. The oil is used extensively to provide one of the main essential fatty acid supplements considered helpful in the cure of angina, brittle nails, eczema, schizophrenia, obesity, and even multiple sclerosis among other diseases.

For such a handsome and extraordinary plant it grow very easily. Indeed, in parts of America it is regarded as a menace in the garden. Elisabeth Sheldon in *A Proper Garden*, calls one of the species, *OE. rosea*, "a lovely stoloniferous menace" and reckons that ten times more money has to be spent to get it out of the garden that was spent to bring it in. If you are afraid that it may creep too far, plant it somewhere in good soil and full sun but where it will not smother everything else. Most varieties divide easily but the low-growing *OE. missouriensis* must be grown from seed.

There are few flower names as evocative as "forget-me-not". "That blue and bright-eyed flowerlet of the brook/Hope's gentle gem, the sweet Forget-me-not" wrote Coleridge in *The Keepsake*, capturing the feelings of generations for this little lovers' flower. Botanically, it is from the genus *Myositis*, Greek for "mouse ear", a name given to plants with pointed leaves.

While it was positively identified in the sixteenth century as belonging to the *Myositis* family, it acquired its present name in the nineteenth century. It has been described as a child of the valleys and marsh lands of Europe, of high value and charming in all its ways. The ability of the plant to keep close to the ground lends itself to many different creative uses in the garden and none better than when mixed with those other late spring flowers, tulips and wallflowers. The forget-me-not plant can be used to great effect in wild gardens, mixed borders and among shrubs, while it can also be happily introduced into large containers and hanging baskets.

Seed should be sown in summer for next spring flowering and takes about two weeks to germinate. The forget-me-not is usually thought of as being blue but there are various other colours, such as pink and white, that have been with us for many years. In wild conditions the plants will seed themselves but in gardens repeat seed sowing is generally necessary. It will grow in most garden soils given partial shade, moisture and a good organic compost, such as leaf mould. It has been selected by the Royal Air Force Association as its floral emblem.

The healers of old must have been grateful when the hollyhock arrived from China around the thirteenth century. Until then the family of plants to which it belonged – the common mallow – had been a weak variety, although associated with a compendium of cures for everything from "moderating the passions" to clearing the stomach and the mind. When the hollyhock arrived in England it was given that name, a derivation of *holy-hock*, because of its healing abilities. It was a large, robust plant, taller than the mallow but with the same medicinal values. Its tall spikes of wide funnel-shaped flowers made it attractive also as an ornamental plant especially in old cottage gardens where it was grown at the back of borders and where height was needed. The hollyhock's botanical name is *Althaea* and there are some twelve hardy annuals, biennials and perennial species. There is a wide range of colours including pink, crimson, scarlet, yellow, white and violet. *A. rosea* is spectacular, often growing to 10 ft/3m with single and double flowers. The single-flowered variety delighted Gertrude Jekyll. She wrote in *Wood and Garden*: "The wide outer petal (a heresy to the florist) makes the flower infinitely more beautiful than the all-over double form that alone is esteemed on the show-table." The foliage is distinctive, being light green, rough and hairy. It makes a useful calming potion for wasp stings when crushed in olive oil and applied immediately.

For best effect, renew plants regularly, otherwise they may fall victims to rust disease. Plants can be grown from seeds grown out-doors in June or July, although many varieties are self-seeding. They are best grown as biennials. Like most plants, the hollyhock responds best to a heavy, rich soil in a sheltered spot but watering is essential during dry periods.

ᘒ Iris ᘓ

Once the iris was a simple blue flower that could be seen growing in the wild by a pond or in a field. Today, while the wild iris is still prevalent, iris plants come in many colours. That is not surprising since the name means "rainbow". In the sixteenth century Lyte described them as "the Dwarffe ireos, the stincking iris and the yellow Iris." Not very complimentary, but for all that the plant developed through the years until now the flowers range in colour from inky black to blue with reds, pinks, purples, yellows, whites in between.

The iris family is a large one – hundreds of hybrids and at least two hundred wild species from *I. alata* to *I. xiphiodes*. The plant originated in all parts of the world; some varieties are heavily scented such as *I. barnume* and some may have the suggestion of a stink. There are two types of plants – bulbous and rhizamatous. Bulbous plants come into flower at different times of the year and need little attention. For gardeners, however, the ones grown from rhizomes are the most eye-catching. These include the small bearded Irises that flower early in spring for a short period and the intermediate group which has more flowers per stem and which puts on a fine show. The most spectacular of all are the tall bearded varieties. They need a sunny spot with good drainage although there are some that live happily in damp lakesides. They should not be planted deeply, and the tops of the rhizomes should be exposed with the roots spread out and facing downwards.

ℭ Jasmine ℰ

One of the most versatile plants growing in the garden, the jasmine flowers in winter, in spring and in summer. It also has one of the most strongly scented flowers. The name comes from the Latin version of the Persian name *Yasmin*. It was introduced to Europe in the sixteenth century and has been popular since then. William Blake suggested "in seed time learn, in harvest teach, in winter enjoy" (*Proverbs of Hell*). He could have been talking about the winter jasmine (*J. nudiflorum*) which clothes bare walls with its starry, golden-yellow flowers, from December to spring, clustering around walls and houses when allowed to wander at will. This is followed by the spring jasmine (*J. polyanthum*), with deep pink fragrant buds. Not quite so hardy as other varieties, it is often grown in cool greenhouses where it must be pruned hard when flowering finishes. In warmer areas, such as the southern counties of England and the south of France, it grows up to 10 ft/3 m high.

J. officinale is the "common" version of the plant. Found growing in old gardens for generations, its white fragrant blossoms make it one of the best climbing shrubs. It twines itself through trees and over bowers in summer growth that can reach a height of 30 ft/9 m and it flowers over a long period. Its summer companion is *J. revolutum*, a loose-growing shrub with an eventual height of about 8 ft/2.4 m with a 5 ft/1.5 m spread. This variety also likes to be close to a wall. The small fragrant yellow flowers show in clusters from June to August. All jasmines need a well-drained and warm site to flourish. Propagation is by nodal cuttings of semi-ripe wood or by layering the shoots, though jasmines can also be raised from seed. The only other care jasmines need is pruning when they have become overgrown.

↞ Lavender ↠

It is hard to tell whether lavender is a shrub, a hedge or a flower. It has been found in gardens for centuries. It has a singular fragrance and a unique history. Before the discoveries of modern science, lavender was used as a bath-additive and a deodorant and its uses in medicine have been wide. As a powerful antiseptic oil, tincture or essence, it has been used to cure cuts, bruises, burns and infections and is supposedly strong enough to kill even diptheria and typhoid bacteria. Naturalists and holistic medicine enthusiasts have placed it high on their plant lists. St Hildegard (1098–1171), a Benedictine abbess, in her famous medical treatise, gave a full page to lavender and its power. In ancient times it was used in bath water (the name is from the Latin *lavere* – to wash). Sachets of lavender were placed in wardrobes and cupboards to enhance, fragrance, and even protect clothes from insects. It was also used as a pleasant-smelling but powerful killer of children's hair parasites. The flowering tips of the shoots and the little blue flowers produce the extracts.

As a garden plant it needs very little cultivation. It should be planted in full sun in a light soil. As the plants grow old, they should be replaced by division or by seeds. To dry, pick the flower heads while they still have colour and before they become too dry. To make lavender oil, put a handful of fresh flowers in a clear container of olive oil and allow it to stand for three days. Strain, and repeat the operation by adding fresh flowers until the oil becomes highly perfumed.

Lily-of-the-Valley, or *convallaria majalis*, is known to have been cultivated for more than five hundred years. In the Vulgate translation of the Song of Songs it is described "I am the Rose of Sharon, and the lily of the valley." It is frequently named in hymns to the Virgin Mary. Herbalists of old used it as a sedative to restore the equilibrium of the nervous system and as a regulator for the heart. The plant has sprays of delicate white bells growing up from clear, green broad leaves and is usually grown in large clumps under woodland or orchard trees, or along a hedge where it can wander at will. Its wanderlust has kept it out of well-tended gardens where its invasive attitude is not appreciated as it sends its roots extensively and is hard to handle once it gets started. It will grow easily, though, in a tub by the front door in the early spring.

The flowers die off quickly but for the short time they show, they have a beautiful fragrance. Lily-of-the-valley needs a moisture-retentive soil and a shady spot. Plants should be left undisturbed if there is space for them to wander but if dividing and transplanting is necessary then they should be lifted when the foliage dies and the plumpest of crowns retained and re-planted immediately. One way of retaining them in a favoured spot is to seal off their roots using a black plastic underlining raised to about the level of the soil.

Nicotania is an annual, the blooms are far from spectacular, it hangs its head during the hours of sunshine and is generally unruly. But when evening arrives the plant comes to life, sweetening the air all around it with a rare perfume. The original and best loved variety *N. alata* has been planted in gardens since the sixteenth century and none of the newer varieties can match its perfume. The flower of this Brazilian half-hardy perennial is greenish-yellow and white within. Nicotiana is also known as the "tobacco" plant and takes its name from Jean Nicot (1530–1600), the French ambassador to Lisbon who introduced tobacco into France. In all, there are over sixty species of half-hardy or tender annual and perennial plants and one of them, *N. tabacum*, is used for the production of tobacco.

New varieties present new colours – a green variety, "Lime Green", being particularly attractive to flower arrangers. Recent varieties of nicotiana look better than the old ones, standing up in sunshine, and presenting a better all-round plant but to offset this the wonderful fragrance is diminished. All varieties need warm, rich and well-drained soil in which to grow effectively. The dead flower-heads should be removed so the plants can continue to produce blooms. Propagation is by seed which must be sown on the surface of the soil under glass. The seedlings need pricking out and hardening off gently before being planted out in late May or early June, depending on the temperature.

✂ Paeony ✂

The paeony is said to be as old as time itself. Its Greek name is possibly derived from Paeon, the physician of the gods, who became so famous for his cures that Hades, god of the underworld, changed him into the plant to ensure his immortality. Pliny wrote that the paeony was the most ancient of plants and various forms of it were well regarded in mediaeval medicine. The best known paeony is *P. officinalis* – the apothecaries' paeony – with its huge blood-red globes of flowers that arrive in late spring. Brought from southern Europe in the sixteenth century, it soon lent itself to plant breeding with double-petalled flowers being hybridised. It is a plant of great diversity, growing in both woodland and cultivated areas. Other forms such as *P. lactiflora* (also known as *P. albiflora*) also grow well, with great clumps of long-lasting foliage which are bowed down to the earth with the weight of huge flower globes. The paeony does not like human intervention and, once growing well, should be left alone. Transplanting takes away its vigour and can cause death.

The paeony arrives in spring with daffodils and tulips, its red, pointed stalks making a lovely accompaniment to the flowering bulbs. The foliage is coarse but elegant and, unless planted in a frosty spot, survives well to last the summer, long after the flowers have fallen. The flowering season is short, especially the yellow Caucasian plant *P. mlokosewitschii*, but the flowers are of great beauty. They are best admired on the bush, although individual blooms placed in a small glass of water provide vivid and short-lived effect. The plants can be propagated by seed but it is a long process to obtain flowering plants. The best method of propagation is to take rooted portions from the outer edges of established clumps.

∽ Pansy ∾

"There's rosemary, that's for remembrance; pray, love, remember: and there is pansies, that's for thoughts," wrote Shakespeare in *Hamlet*. Milton in *Lycidas* described the pansy as "freaked with jet", Edgar Allen Poe wrote of "beautiful Puritan Pansies" and Shakespeare called it "Love in Idleness". The French novelist Colette, who wrote so many superb evocations of gardens and flowers, saw the pansy being "imbued with a dusting of constellations". For such a modest little flower, the pansy has enchanted many gardeners with its constancy and ability to grow. The Floral Code has always described it as a symbol of remembrance. Who has not been intrigued by the multi-coloured faces, whiskery and velvet, of its blooms?

In botanical terms it comes from the Viola family (*V. x wittrockiana*), largely from the *V. tricolour* line which was known as the "heartease", possibly from the medicinal use of the wild pansy for cleaning the blood. It was also called the "garden-gate", for the welcome it gives when grown inside a gate.

Today it is one of the most versatile and easily grown plants for garden, window box, hanging basket or container of any kind. As a ground-cover it is invaluable, while in rock gardens it provides fine splashes of colour. Pansies can grow in any garden or balcony all year long with the winter-flowering varieties from to multi-coloured summer varieties. The plant is mainly biennial but will grow uninterrupted for many years, given good watering and some feeding and grown in a lightly shaded and well-drained place. The plants must be deadheaded regularly or will fade away through seed setting. The unassuming pansy always lends charm to a garden.

The passion flower is very distinctive. A native of tropical America, the early missionaries in the forests of Brazil associated it with Christ's crucifixion and took it as a message that one day Brazil would be converted to Christianity. In the extraordinary flower they saw a corona that for them was the crown of thorns, the five anthers representing the five wounds, and the three styles they saw as the three nails; they saw ten apostles here too (minus Peter and Judas) and many other signs associated with the Passion. The foliage also carried a message. Shaped like an open hand, it was taken as a welcoming sign.

While there are some five hundred species, the one associated with most gardens is *P. caerulea*, which makes a vigorous evergreen and often wildly tangled climber when grown in a warm, sunny place. The flowers are large and beautiful with greenish-white star-shaped sepals. Inside is a corona made up of filaments which are blue at the top and white in the centre, shading to deep purplish blue at the base. It grows very effectively at the base of a south-facing hedge or, preferably, against a wall where the reflected heat helps the wood to ripen. In cool spots the tips may be killed by frosts but the main stems, once established, are quite hardy. The added protection of a covering of straw or bracken for the roots will help ensure its survival. It should be planted in late spring in well-drained soil. Spring pruning should be hard with all dead wood cut out at the base and side shoots shortened back. Flowers appear between June and September and are followed by bright orange-coloured, egg-shaped fruits which, although edible, are not very palatable. The passion fruit found in greengrocers is grown in the West Indies.

❦ Primula ❧

It is said that no garden is quite complete without the rose and the same might be said of the primula, the polyanthus or the primrose, all of which come from a family of great aptitude and beauty. These plants grow in shaded places, in sunny rock gardens, in woodland, in bogland – almost anywhere the gardener or nature wishes them to grow. It is hard to classify the beautiful little hedge primrose as *Primula vulgaris*; much more appropriate is the Latin *prima rose*, the first rose to mark the arrival of spring. The sixteenth century writers, Beaumont and Fletcher, wrote in *Two Noble Kinsmen*: 'Primrose, first born child of Ver, Merry Spring-time's harbinger.' Writers of every generation have described the beauty of the little flower. In the eighteenth century Oliver Goldsmith wrote in *The Deserted Village*: 'Sweet as the primrose peeps beneath the thorn.'

The dividing line between the primrose, the polyanthus and the primula is unclear and the family contains more than a hundred varieties. The plants can be found in perennial, annual and biennial types; some are alpine, some are tall, some can even be grown indoors for a time before being discarded. Many of the garden primulas are short-lived and some favoured plants must be tenderly treated when they are divided to give new plants. Starting from seed can often be erratic and may require a cold frame or a greenhouse in which to have the seeds germinate. Grow the plants in sun or partial shade in a fertile soil that stays moist – the secret of success.

ભ Sweet Pea ∾

The summer fragrance of the sweet pea wafts its perfumed loveliness through the air no matter the time of day or night. A native of Sicily, it became known in our gardens in 1700 and since then has been called "the most precious annual" grown. It comes from a fairly large family whose botanical name is *Lathyrus*, a Greek word for pea. This group includes everlasting and miniature types but the sweet pea (*L. odoratus*) is the queen. The fragrance is what makes the sweet pea special. Many gardeners prefer the everlasting pea which repeats growth year after year and even looks like sweet pea, but does not have the same fragrance.

The sweet pea is the most accommodating of garden annuals. It can be grown to cover many garden mistakes where its tall growth and wonderful blooms will clothe garden canes to an almost blanket effect. As a climber, it will race up poles or along walls or fences. It will twine into awkward shrubs and make them things of beauty, or cover a wigwam of poles set in the back of a border. And there are few plants that can give such a marvellous return as a hedge of sweet pea. The colour range is all-embracing from pastel to strong single colours and many bicolours. Each year sees new varieties on the market but finding some of the older ones can be very gratifying. A variety like Painted Lady, which was first listed a century ago, is still high on the plantsmen's lists for its carmine-rose and white heavily scented blooms. Easy to grow when given good, well-composted ground, sweet pea delights in a sunny spot and must be given support on which to grow. Plants are best started in a greenhouse in September to October, but seeds can be planted in situ from March to May. For continuity of bloom, flowers must be picked early and regularly.

ଔ Sweet William ଷ

Dianthus barbatus is the botanical name for Sweet William, one of the easiest to grow and showiest of garden flowers. It is hardy, vigorous, cheery and obliging, with flowers in every colour. It is a plant that will grow easily anywhere … from seeds, root division or even cuttings and is not easily afflicted by diseases or pests. Its abilities to continue to grow when left undisturbed can be seen in old castle and garden walls where it has naturalized. It seems to have always been a resident in our gardens but the version that we know today is only two hundred years old. It was a staple plant in the Victorian garden and even today it is rarely missing from cottage gardens. Sweet William roots easily, sending up new plants everywhere and can generally be found in multicoloured clumps of bright blooms. Although it is a member of the *Dianthus* family, it is quite unlike the rest of the family, being much different in flower production to the pinks and the annual carnation, its immediate cousins.

A close look at the densely packed heads of flowers will reveal miniature, individual carnation-like blooms. It is this mass of flowers in a huge variety of colours that makes it so distinctive. While it is possible to purchase single colour varieties, it is the old-fashioned white-eyed varieties that make the best splash of colour. These colours vary from flower to flower in rich shadings even within a single head. Plants from seed sown in spring should be put out into their permanent spots in September for flowering the following summer. They grow best in a sunny spot in light soil with a touch of lime.